GSD&M • i d e a u n i v e r s i t y p r e s s
a u s t i n , t e x a s

THIS BOOK IS FOR ALL KIDS, BUT ESPECIALLY MY SISTER LIBBY.

LIBBY DIED.

BY JACK SIMON, WHEN HE WAS 5 YEARS OLD.
ILLUSTRATED BY HIS MOM, ANNETTE SIMON,
WHEN SHE WAS 36 YEARS OLD.

DID YOU

for our moms and dads.
for Kent. for Grant.
for all our family, especially Libby.
-Jack & Annette

Mighty Max® is a trademark owned by Mattel, Inc., used with permission.

hear me?

SHE DIED.

aND WHEN YOU

even Have To (

DIE, YOU DON'T

T CHICKEN POX.

ve FOOD. YOU DON'T even need FOOD.

I'M HUNGRY.

LIBBY WAS JUST SO SICK, NO DOCTORS COULD HELP H

SHE'S TH

mom,

WHAT IF   LIBBY WAS YOUR FIRST BABY, AND I WAS THE MIDDLE K

SO SHE HAD TO DIE.

SO SHE DID.

SHE'S THE FIRST ONE IN OUR FAMILY TO DIE.
FIRST ONE TO BE WITH THE ANGELS.

WOULD IT HAVE BEEN ME?   WOULD I BE DEAD NOW?

WELL, WHEN
JUST PUT MY
SUPERHERO
FIGURES ON
SO I CAN BR
UP TO heaven
and we car
WITH THEM

MAYBE SOMEO

I DIE,

ACTION
MY CHEST
G THEM
WITH ME
PLAY

Yeah, if i could ask libby about being in heaven

You're dea

and how do ane
wings out of ti
do you move the
with wing insti
wouldn't it be funny if you had wings coming o

O HOW EXACTLY DO YOU LIVE?

LS GROW THOSE
IR BACKS? HOW
m? DO THEY COME
JCTIONS?
YOUR EYEBALLS? OR ON YOUR BUTT? hahahaha

AND IF YOU DON'T NEED YOUR BODY ANYMOR

e THERE JUST HEADS FLOATING AROUND?

mom, WILL LIBBY Have THE same fac

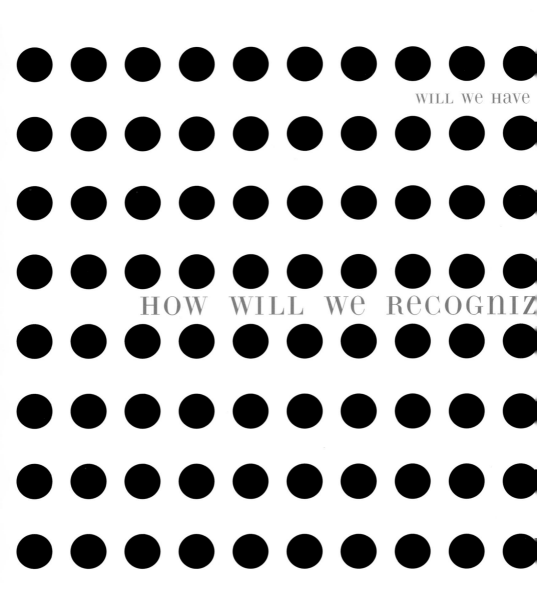

WILL we have

HOW WILL we RECOGNIZ

D CLOTHES ON WHEN WE SEE HER AS AN ANGEL?

ᴋ ALL THE ANGELS WHICH ONES ARE NAMED LIBBY?

ER?

DO ANGELS

SLEEP? DO

STAY AWAKE

AND EVERY

ever go to

THEY

every day

night?

I WOULD LIKE TO ASK HE

LIKE HOW MUCH DOES SH

a sad question, too...

ove us and miss us.

HEY, LIBBY.... DID YOU GET THE BALLOONS W

ew up for your birthday?

in Hea

are you

as you

on ea

en,

as BIG

were

TH?

WOW.

now you know what god looks like.

WHEN YOU DIE, YOU CA

AND DOORS AND

EVEN LIBBY. WHEN SHE WA

MIXED UP. SHE COULDN

CRAWL ANYWHERE, BU

FLOAT

FLOAT THROUGH WALLS

STUFF THAT YOU CAN'T DO NOW.

ALIVE, HER BONES WERE

EVEN HUG ANYONE OR

HOW SHE CAN EVEN

THROUGH WALLS.

I KNOW! IT'S LIKE ALADDIN'S GENIE.

WHEN YOU'RE ON EARTH, YOUR BODY'S LIKE YOUR MAST

AND WHEN YOU DIE, YOU'RE se

F

R e e

RIGHT, LIF

and since you can now...

GIVE GOD A HUG FOR ME, TOO.

BY!